People Jesus Met

Retold by Owen Cole and Judith Lowndes

Illustrated by Eric Rowe

Heinemann Educational Publishers
Halley Court, Jordan Hill, Oxford OX2 8EJ

MADRID ATHENS PARIS
FLORENCE PRAGUE WARSAW
PORTSMOUTH NH CHICAGO SAO PAULO
SINGAPORE TOKYO MELBOURNE AUCKLAND
IBADAN GABORONE JOHANNESBURG

First published 1995

95 96 97 98 99 10 9 8 7 6 5 4 3 2 1

British Library Cataloguing in Publication Data
A catalogue record for this book is available from the British Library

Starter Pack
1 of each of 12 titles: ISBN 0 435 01066 2

Library Hardback Edition
People Jesus Met: ISBN 0 431 07758 4
1 of each of 12 titles: ISBN 0 431 07763 0

Designed by Sue Vaudin; printed and bound in Hong Kong

Acknowledgements
Back cover photograph:
Sonia Halliday Photographs

Jesus lived long ago.
He told people all about God.
Many people changed after they
had met Jesus.

The stories about the people that
Jesus met are in the Bible.
The Bible is a special book for
Christians.
Here are two of the stories.

The Fishermen

One day Jesus was by the sea.
Many people tried to get close to
hear him talk.
They were pushing and pushing.

It was so crowded that Jesus got into a fishing boat.
He asked the fishermen to push the boat out into the sea a little way.

Jesus spoke to the people from the boat.

When he had finished talking he told the fishermen to put their nets in the water to catch some fish.

“We have been fishing all night.
It is no good,” said the fishermen.

But they put their nets into
the water anyway.

They were surprised!

Their nets were full.

There were lots of fish!

Jesus said to the fishermen,
"From now on you will be
catching men.
Follow me!"

So they did.

When they got to the shore they left their nets and followed Jesus.

Jesus Meets a Rich Man

This story is about a man called
Zacchaeus.
Zacchaeus was very rich.

Zacchaeus had a job that made him rich.

He collected tax money from people.

Everyone had to pay tax.

Zacchaeus heard that Jesus was
coming to his town.
Lots of people had come to see Jesus.

Zacchaeus was a little man.

There were so many people that

Zacchaeus could not see Jesus.

Zacchaeus ran to a tree and
climbed up into it.
He waited for Jesus to come by.

When Jesus came to the tree he
looked up.
"Hurry down, Zacchaeus," said Jesus.
"I must stay in your house today."

Zacchaeus was very happy.
He came down from the tree and
took Jesus to his house.

Some people were angry.
They said, “Zacchaeus is a bad man.
Jesus has gone to the house of a
bad man.”

At his house Zacchaeus said to Jesus, “I am going to give away half of all I have to poor people.”

Then he said, "If I have cheated anyone
I will pay them back that money.
Then I will give them four times more."

Jesus was pleased with him.
Zacchaeus became one of
Jesus' followers.